Ha!
Monster
JOKES
A Buddy Book
by Ima Laffin
Buddy BOOKS
Jokes

VISIT US AT

www.abdopub.com

Published by ABDO Publishing Company, 4940 Viking Drive, Suite 622, Edina, Minnesota 55435.

Printed in the United States.

Edited by: Sarah Tieck
Contributing Editors: Matt Ray, Michael P. Goecke
Graphic Design: Deborah Coldiron
Illustrations by: Deborah Coldiron and Maria Hosley

Library of Congress Cataloging-in-Publication Data

Laffin, Ima, 1970-
Monster jokes / Ima Laffin.
p. cm. — (Jokes)
Includes index.
ISBN 1-59197-623-5
1. Monsters—Juvenile humor. 2. Wit and humor, Juvenile. [1. Monsters—Humor. 2. Riddles. 3. Jokes.] I. Title. II. Series.

PN6231.M665L34 2004
818'.5402—dc22

2003069304

Why is it interesting to study mummies?

Because you can get so wrapped up in them.

How do you stop a monster from digging up your garden?

Take his shovel away.

Why are a monster's fingers never more than 11 inches long?

Twelve inches make a foot.

How can you tell if there's a monster in your closet?

You can't shut the door!

How did the monster cure his sore throat?

He spent all day gargoyling.

What do you get if you cross the Loch Ness monster with a shark?

Loch jaws.

What happened to the wolf that fell into the washing machine?

It became a wash-and-werewolf.

How do you keep an ugly monster in suspense?

I'll tell you tomorrow . . .

Did you hear about the monster who sent his picture to a lonely hearts club?

They said no one was that lonely!

Did you hear about the day Romeo monster met Juliet monster?

It was love at first fright.

What do monsters read in the newspaper?

The Horror-scope.

What do you call a one-eyed monster who rides a motorcycle?

Cycle-ops!

Why doesn't Dracula have any friends?

Because he's a pain in the neck.

Why didn't the monster use toothpaste?

He said his teeth weren't loose.

What does a headless horseman ride?

A night-mare.

What do you get if you cross a giant monster with a penguin?

I don't know, but its tuxedo is tight.

What did the Loch Ness monster say to his friend?

Long time no sea.

What do you call a mouse who can pick up a monster?

Sir.

What do you get if you cross a monster with a kangaroo?

Big holes all over Australia.

What happened to the two mad vampires?

They went a little batty.

What do you get if you cross a monster with a scout?

A monster that scares old ladies across the street.

Did you hear about the monster who had eight arms?

He said they came in handy.

Did you hear about the monster who took the train home?

His mother made him give it back.

The police are looking for a monster with one eye.

Why don't they use two?

What do you give a seasick monster?

Plenty of room!

What do you get if you cross a monster with a watchdog?

Very nervous mail carriers!

What do you get if you cross a monster with a pigeon?

Lots of very worried walkers!

What happens if a big, hairy monster sits in front of you at the theater?

You miss most of the movie!

What can a monster do that you can't do?

Count up to 25 on his fingers.

Who brings monsters their babies?

Franken-stork.

Did you hear about the monster burglar who fell in the cement mixer?

Now he's a hardened criminal.

What is big, slimy, and ugly—and very blue?

A monster holding its breath.

What do vampires cross the sea in?

Blood vessels.

How do you stop a werewolf from howling in the back of a car?

Put him in the front seat.

What did the big, hairy monster do when he lost a hand?

He went to the secondhand shop.

Why was the big, hairy, two-headed monster at the top of the class at school?

Because two heads are better than one.

What happens when monsters hold beauty contests?

Nobody wins.

What do you do with a green monster?

Put it in the sun until it ripens!

Why was the monster standing on his head?

He was turning things over in his mind.

What do you get if you cross a long-fanged, purple-spotted monster with a cat?

How do you greet a three-headed monster?

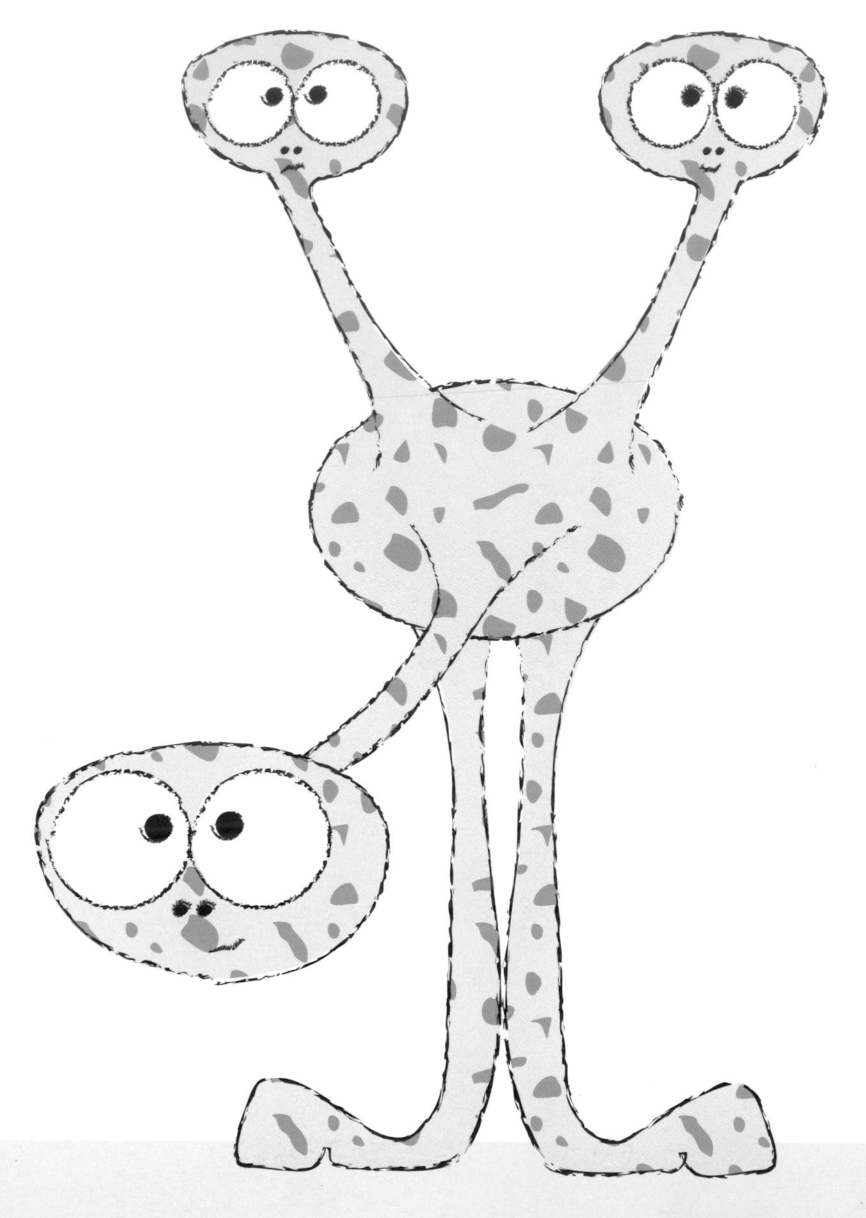

Hello! Hello! Hello!

What did the werewolf write on his holiday cards?

Best vicious of the season.

What do you call a dog owned by Dracula?

A bloodhound.

What does a polite monster say when he meets you for the first time?

Pleased to eat you!

How do you talk to a giant?

Use big words.

Why does the little girl monster think her brother was born upside down?

His nose runs, and his feet smell.

Did you hear about the monster with five legs?

His pants fit him like a glove.

What is a monster's favorite game?

Swallow the leader.

What do you get if you cross a plum with a man-eating monster?

A purple people eater.

What does a boy monster do when a girl monster rolls her eyes at him?

He picks them up and rolls them back.

Visit ABDO Publishing Company on the World Wide Web. Joke Web sites for children are featured on our Book Links page. These links are monitored and updated to provide the silliest information available.

www.abdopub.com